WONDER WINGS
BUTTERFLY COLORING BOOK

Jessica Mazurkiewicz

Dover Publications, Inc.
Mineola, New York

In this enchanting coloring book you will find thirty illustrations of butterflies—but not the kind found in nature! Instead, artist Jessica Mazurkiewicz has fashioned whimsical variations of the insect, giving them human faces and beautifully patterned wings. So get your crayons, markers, and colored pencils ready as you prepare to enter the world of wonder wings!

Bibliographical Note

Wonder Wings Butterfly Coloring Book is a new work, first published by Dover Publications, Inc., in 2015.

International Standard Book Number
ISBN-13: 978-0-486-78937-8
ISBN-10: 0-486-78937-3

Manufactured in the United States by RR Donnelley
78937303   2015
www.doverpublications.com